TEN PRAYER NUGGETS

Practical ways to lead others in corporate prayer

Lloyd Jansen van Vuuren

authorHOUSE®

AuthorHouse™
1663 Liberty Drive
Bloomington, IN 47403
www.authorhouse.com
Phone: 833-262-8899

Published by AuthorHouse 09/08/2021

ISBN: 978-1-6655-3726-1 (sc)
ISBN: 978-1-6655-3727-8 (e)

Endorsements

"Lloyd has taken his years of experience in different church settings, coupled with his own constant personal devotion in prayer, and collated these 'nuggets' which are punchy, accessible, applicable and ultimately will help you pray and lead others in prayer. Take them, apply them, and grow through them." – Hugh Pearce, Pastor at Redeemer Church Colchester (redeemerchurchcolchester.org)

"The Nuggets have been a useful succinct guide for those leading prayer in our house group - I believe that they would be helpful in any prayer meeting. Books abound on how to preach, but I can't recall instruction on leading in prayer. I have found Nuggets to be a useful succinct guide." – Guy Pembroke, Lead Trainer at Path of Disciples (Pathofdisciples.org)

"Lloyd is a man with a passion for the Lord and a calling to set God's people praying. These nuggets bring practical wisdom and godly insight together and will be a valuable asset to any group or church seeking to grow in praying together." – Steven Anderson, One of the Church Leaders at Glasgow City Church (glasgowcitychurch.com), Leader of 'Breakthrough in the Spirit' Ministry and Leader of a city-wide prayer initiative across Glasgow for years.

"Many books have been published on the topic of prayer, and some are proven classics. But guidelines on corporate prayer are disturbingly rare - remarkable given the significance of group prayer, and also the added dynamics incurred by such engagement. I know no one more qualified to write on this topic than Lloyd van Vuuren. With a passion for, and sensitivity in, group prayer, Lloyd is well experienced in leading corporate intercession. I wish every church in the land would lay hold on this short collection of prayer 'nuggets' - invaluable advice for all believers." – Tom Lennie, Revival historian; author of 'Glory in the Glen', 'Land of Many Revivals' and 'Scotland Ablaze' (truerevival.net)

"These nuggets represent an essential foundation for the people of God in this generation: in them we find keys to intimacy with the Lord and a vision to see nations change." – Akhtar Shah, Leadership Team at All Nations Movement of Churches (allnationsmovement.org), Founder and Leader of The Foundry, Founder of Dreams Lab.

"Prayer is often an unmined commodity for Christians that is of exceptional value. I highly commend Lloyd's resource as it will fuel worship and mission! Lloyd's work is practical, biblical and of great importance for us to hear in these days." – Dr Desmond Henry, Director of Global Network of Evangelists at the Luis Palau Association (evangelist.global)

"Drawing on his own experience of leading prayer groups and encouraging corporate prayer, Lloyd's little booklet is full of golden nuggets - practical yet also spiritual - a great resource for anyone wishing to encourage their home group or church fellowship to 'step out of the boat' and embark on the corporate prayer adventure!" — Alistair Barton, Director of Pray for Scotland (prayforscotland.org.uk) and Elder, Kirkliston Parish Church (kirklistonparish.org).

"This is a handy little booklet, giving lots of themes and ideas for corporate prayer. It will be especially useful to anyone leading or planning corporate prayer meetings. The Prayer meeting is vital in the life of every local church. We need all the help we can get to make those meetings vibrant, biblical, powerful and effective." — Mike Betts, Leader of Relational Mission (relationalmission.org), Founder of Prayers of Many (prayersofmany.org)

Contents

Introduction

The 'prayer nuggets' were developed through hosting prayer meetings over several years, making many mistakes along the way and, in the process, turning some of the lessons learnt into short and accessible tips, with the intention of encouraging and strengthening others to learn to meaningfully pray together too. These nuggets are not a methodology, or a checklist, but instead are intended as short and practical guidance or tips that should encourage, embed, and strengthen a culture of corporate prayer in any local church. Whilst the following nuggets relate primarily to corporate prayer, they also touch on and encourage private prayer.

The priority of prayer: Jesus prioritised prayer [Matt 26:36, Luke 6:12, Luke 18:1] and this meant he sometimes disappointed people in order to spend time in prayer [Matthew 14:23, Mark 1:35-37, Luke 5:15-16].

When the people of God desire to meet with Him in prayer and prioritise time with Him, both individually and corporately in a local church setting, very soon prayer will become the 'engine room' of the local church. This allows space where God can speak, individuals can mature, leaders can emerge, and entire communities can be set on fire for God's plans and His great purposes.

Jesus described His Father's house as a house of prayer [Matthew 21:13, Mark 11:17]. He could have pointed to many things that would characterise His people and their gathered community – but

He chose to name prayer as the defining feature. In a similar way, prayer to our Heavenly Father is one vital activity from which most other aspects of church life can be nourished, flow from and grow in, as a wonderful side effect.

When a local church prioritises corporate prayer, the whole body begins to stir and awaken to what God is doing. Corporate prayer could be the single most vital activity that will synchronise hearts in a church community, clarify and impart vision, and allow a church to sense, hear, and confirm corporately what God might be saying.

Private prayer fuels corporate prayer and devotion to God: Elijah was a great Old Testament prophetic character, known for his courageous and powerful ministry. Elijah mentions the LORD of hosts "before whom he stood" [1 Kings 18:15]. Evidently, he had spent enough time before God as an individual, that he was no longer anxious and afraid of what people thought of him or could do to him.

The problems that had previously discouraged him, he saw shrink before the greatness and splendour of God Almighty. So too, when God's people have been with Him in private and then come together in prayer, the gathered people of God will come alive to the things of God as their faith is stirred, God speaks, and prophetic activity is given space and encouraged.

What about 'Unanswered' prayer? Whilst a rapid response to prayer is encouraging or even faith building, a more subtle danger may be getting 'answers' too soon without meeting with God through persevering prayer and having our hearts warmed to His purposes and drawn into His presence. The glory of prayer is getting into the presence of God Almighty – our Heavenly Father. When God does not appear to respond immediately, there is still the need to keep pressing in together and keep praying, and there is then the opportunity to hear God speaking about a multitude of other things 'along the way'.

By not putting the phone down as soon as the business of the call has concluded, and instead tarrying, we learn to see things from God's point of view. God is far greater than an 'answering machine' – He wants our devotion, our hearts and even our lives [Deuteronomy 6:5]. God wants His people to see Him and to be changed from one degree of glory to another, ultimately becoming more like Him. [2 Cor 3:18]

It must also be noted that we may never fully understand, on this side of eternity, why God decides on a particular outcome or why some prayers are answered differently to how we would expect or strongly desire.

Nugget 1: Corporately praying the promises of God

Prayer feeds off the glorious promises which God has made to His people. By immersing ourselves in what God has said, times of prayer become exciting journeys of discovery and wonder at what God might remind us about when we gather. By starting with the great and glorious promises of God, any corporate gathering to pray launches into the very throne room of heaven. Expectations are raised, faith is stirred, and everyone present becomes more alert to what God might be saying to His gathered people.

God works through promise-backed prayer to nurture, grow, and mature our faith. By reading, declaring, and rejoicing in the promises God has already made, we are reminded that, *"Not one word of all the good promises that the LORD has made to [His People] has failed; all have come to pass."* [Joshua 21:45.]

When we start a time of corporate prayer, immersed in the promises of God, the atmosphere will be thanksgiving, soaked in praise and alive with wonder at who our God is, because of what He has said and already done and will continue to do for us.

"A promise is a note written in His own hand, and He will acknowledge His own handwriting." ~ Herbert Lockyer.

"The promises of God should be the basis of all our prayers, for they are alike our warrant for asking and our security for receiving." ~ W.C. Proctor.

'I will put my law within them, and I will write it on their hearts. And I will be their God, and they shall be my people... I will forgive their iniquity, and I will remember their sin no more.' ~ Jeremiah 31:33-34

Nugget 2: Corporately pray the truths of the Bible

Consider sections in the Bible that are rich in the glorious truths about our God, the Gospel, the Cross, the saving power of Christ, and whose we are, along with who we are in Him. Often, after hearing truth declared or prayed, people start to awaken and begin to soak and soar in all that God is to us, has won for us, and is doing in us. By declaring the truths of scripture, a time of prayer can be used to teach essential doctrine. The most illuminating moments of reading the Bible can be on our knees with others.

'Faith comes from hearing and hearing through the word of Christ.' ~ Romans 10:17.

If we believe this, we will do well to give space for God's word to be proclaimed and prayed as we meet to pray together to stir up one another's faith.

Consider for a moment, that we are justified, have peace with God in Christ, and have access to God's abundant grace which we stand in right now; and now too we get to rejoice in hope, a hope that is grounded in the glory of God himself.

These wonderful truths are for all of God's people to know and live in today and can be found very easily on every page of the Bible: *'Since we have been justified by faith, we have peace with God through our Lord Jesus Christ. Through him we have also obtained access by faith into this grace in which we stand, and we rejoice in hope of the glory of God.'* ~ Romans 5:1-2.

If you are ever wondering what or how to pray for someone or a situation, your own Bible can be the best prayer manual. Open it up and pray it out, even out loud if you can.

Nugget 3: Corporately pray the prayers of the Bible

The Bible records, throughout salvation history, a great number of individuals calling out to God in the depths of despair, ecstatic joy, and everything between. We can use their inspired prayers and words to launch us into a greater trajectory and rhythm of prayer, by reading out loud their prayers from the Bible, or else through making some aspects of their prayers into our own words, by adapting them to our circumstances and situation. For example, by placing our names or those of our churches into the fabric of the recorded prayers.

Start by using the prayers from the book of Psalms, which is a collection of prayers, laments and songs as a launch-pad for any corporate prayer gathering. The Psalms are filled with thanksgiving and praise along with an upward God-focus. They guide our hearts to look up and become more aware and alive to what God may want to say. The Psalms are especially helpful when everyone feels a bit 'flat' and could do with drawing on the inspired words and historic faith of those who have run the race before.

As Jesus died on the cross, He prayed Psalm 31:5 *"Into your hand I commit my Spirit."* directing us to make use of the prayers of scripture in our correspondence with our Heavenly Father. Importantly, this includes our laments, complaints, and concerns, as we see so honestly portrayed often in the Psalms.

Nugget 4: Adapt any appropriate verse into a corporate cry to God

Take any verse or portion of the Bible and fashion it into a prayer. For example, Psalm 23: "The Lord is My Shepherd". We can give thanks together to God that he is OUR Shepherd, that He is leading US, and similarly use each phrase as a springboard for thanksgiving and praise.

When we use the Bible to pray, we are simultaneously preaching to ourselves, whilst reminding ourselves of what God has already said from his Word, and we are also talking to God!

'The whole word of God is of use to direct us in prayer, and how can we express ourselves in better language to God than that of His own Spirit.' ~ Matthew Henry

'All Scripture is breathed out by God and profitable for teaching, for reproof, for correction, and for training in righteousness, that the man of God may be complete, equipped for every good work.' ~ 2 Timothy 3:16-17

Nugget 5: Praying together 'For the glory of God'

When Jesus taught his disciples to pray, he started off with *"Our Father in Heaven, hallowed be your name."* [Matthew 6:9, Luke 11:2]

When we start by considering God's glory, it puts our gaze and our hearts on our all-good Heavenly Father, before we even ask or mention a request or get going on a 'list'. This helps to remind us of whose we are, who we are, and what we are doing – speaking to the One who created and holds the entire universe in balance!

When we consider first the goodness, greatness, and glory of God, and begin to adore and love Him, longing to see His name exalted, His fame promoted and His kingdom extended, suddenly our hearts are stirred, and prayer moves from a task or duty to an incredible privilege and delight.

'Not to us, O LORD, not to us, but to your name give glory, for the sake of your steadfast love and your faithfulness.' ~ Psalm 115:1

Nugget 6: Instead of only talking, try to mostly pray

To ensure we spend most of our time praying and not 'just' talking to each other in a corporate prayer meeting, consider cultivating a habit of keeping any talking brief as well as turning any 'prayer updates' directly into prayer. Try to speak about any circumstances to God together rather than launching into a detailed conversation to the gathered community, leaving very little time to pray about the situation. Notice how it may be 'explained' sufficiently as you pray, enabling others to hear what is most precious, important, or of greatest concern without needing to be given the precise details and they will be able to also pray over the situation. When we do this, it avoids spending precious gathered time hearing about things that we could instead be praying for and potentially run out of time to adequately pray through.

There are exceptions to this, of course, where a very *brief* update will serve the resulting prayer time well; but make them the exception rather than the norm.

To make prayer meetings meaningful, powerful and alive to what God is doing, meeting hosts need the discipline to not let it slip into a social gathering with a bit of prayer tacked on at the end or only if there is time. By prioritising social gatherings at other times, getting together to pray can be focussed on prayer.

Introductions: Instead of feeling the need to have a lengthy time of small talk or an icebreaker at the start of the prayer meeting to 'warm' people up or get to know each other, consider allowing time to chat at the end of the corporate prayer time, this ensures that prayer remains the priority and is not swamped by conversation.

Nugget 7: Try to keep on topic, allow space for others to participate and God to speak

Keeping on topic: When we pray with others, consider it a conversation we might have with a group of friends. By treating prayer as a group conversation before God, we move together and the discussion flows naturally, in the presence of, and with, God.

When we take time to pray through issues together before rushing on to another topic, prayer times will become alive and fresh, not feeling like a rushed conversation, thereby enabling greater participation by all. Try to keep the theme moving in a similar direction, to avoid bouncing around between very different topics and going 'off-track'. Times of corporate prayer can be greatly enhanced and more powerful when time is deliberately allowed for individuals to 'linger' where God may be trying to speak into a particular issue, before gently moving on when the time is appropriate.

Allow space: Consider allowing brief (*Note: only very brief.*) times of silence to enable others to 'jump in' and not feel shut out of the group conversation. If, as the prayer meeting leader, you sense that someone wants to pray, but maybe just needs a tiny nudge or a gap to pray out, try inviting them to pray out loud with a bit of guidance (i.e., would you like to pray into a particular situation?) to grow their confidence. However, avoid embarrassing someone who you do not know well enough and who may not be ready to publicly pray before others, even in a small group.

Silence to listen and hear God: It must be noted that a 'comfortable' silence to listen to God and hear His gentle voice in a reflective and unrushed manner is a powerful way of inviting the Holy Spirit into any corporate prayer gathering. Playing or listening to worship music can help create an atmosphere of near-silence and encourage individuals to seek God and engage in listening to Him, without the murmur of voices as a distraction. Allow such times of listening to worship music, silence (or near-silence) to be natural and, in a gentle but confident way, encourage others to become comfortable with both short or more lengthy silence. Whilst some silence is useful, try to avoid a prolonged and 'uncomfortable' silence, which would be very unnatural in any other setting and can often be the primary reason prayer meetings falter and fail to gain momentum in the long run. Additionally, do not try to 'drive' a time of corporate prayer or nervously fill silence for the sake of it by just saying or praying anything.

Nugget 8: Try to keep prayers short and punchy, and encourage 'agreement' in prayer

Short prayers generally encourage wider participation and when everyone is contributing, it is engaging and 'alive', and no one is left out or behind. Long prayers, in contrast, can drone on and draw the energy, life, and purpose from a corporate prayer gathering. It is very important for the prayer meeting leader to deal with individuals who pray incredibly long prayers and seem unaware of their length and more importantly of the need to allow others to participate in a time of gathered prayer. This can be done through gentle hints and reminders during the gathered prayer time, to keep prayers relatively brief, or else it can be dealt with alone afterwards where it can be discussed in confidence and explored and explained in more depth. If individuals are not taught to allow space for others, very quickly momentum will be lost, and the culture of prayer can become a time when personal agendas are aired and only a few dominant individuals pray. The idea is to get everyone praying together, not a small group of prayer warriors only.

Caveat: There are exceptions to keeping prayers short; for example, when an individual with a recognised prophetic or prayer gifting begins an anointed prayer that everyone tunes into and 'agrees' with. Praying regularly with a similar group in our local churches helps us to learn and grow together and know when someone is hearing from God or under a particular anointing.

Encourage people to intentionally 'agree' in some way, maybe by occasionally saying 'amen' or 'yes Lord' when something in the prayer resonates or in whatever way is appropriate to keep involved, rather than just listening in silence as one individual prays. By agreeing in prayer, we encourage the person praying and stir our own faith as we engage in the prayer conversation, making their prayer our own. The prayer meeting leader can help embed this, by providing an example to fellow congregants, to demonstrate how it can be a natural way of participation in corporate prayer without becoming a distraction and drowning out the individual(s) praying.

'ONE THING have I asked of the LORD, that will I seek after: that I may dwell in the house of the LORD all the days of my life, to gaze upon the beauty of the LORD and to inquire in his temple.' ~ Psalm 27:4

Nugget 9: Simultaneous corporate prayer

All praying together, 'at the same time', can be a wonderfully 'economical' way to involve everyone and encourage participation by those less likely to pray aloud in front of others. This can be literally 'all together' as a large gathering or else breaking into smaller groups to all pray together as separate groups. From experience, one of the most mentioned fears about corporate prayer is having to pray in front of other people. By all praying together, everyone becomes lost in the 'hum' of group prayer, in just the same way in a choir setting, that an individual choir member's voice is drowned out by the overall choir singing and the volume of all the voices combined.

Praying simultaneously could be the singular most practical and powerful ingredient to getting a church praying corporately (and privately too as a result) and assisting individuals to conquer their 'fear of prayer', when done wisely and sensitively.

When a time of simultaneous group prayer is led well, people will often feel comfortable to pray out on the back of it, having encountered God and heard Him speak to them personally.

'...they lifted their voices together to God and said, "Sovereign Lord, who made the heavens, the earth, and the sea and everything in them."' ~ Acts 4:24.

If the Holy Spirit has given you the gift and ability to pray in tongues, doing so together can be a great way to start an early morning prayer gathering, when no one wants to 'break-the-ice' or all present are still feeling half asleep, and there is a particular need for help in prayer as promised by the Holy Spirit.

Nugget 10: Corporate prayer helps us really get to know each other

A great way to really get to know people is by praying together and discerning through their prayers, their heart, and concern for certain issues. There may be no other way more powerful, so uniting, and conducive to growing a church's love, devotion, and care for each member, than praying together.

When praying in a group setting, encourage natural conversational etiquette, by, for example, praying in a normal voice rather than in a solemn or 'different' voice and being quick to pray rather than leaving long, awkward silences. In general, consider what would be 'normal' and 'acceptable' when having an engaging conversation with friends and allow the same 'norms' to flavour times of corporate prayer. After all, prayer is simply talking to and hearing from God. The more natural and normal the prayer times are, the more the hearts and minds of the members of a local church will feel drawn together.

By praying together, a church comes together and stays together.

'But you, beloved, building yourselves up in your most holy faith and praying in the Holy Spirit, keep yourselves in the love of God, waiting for the mercy of our Lord Jesus Christ that leads to eternal life.' ~ Jude 1:20-21

About the Author

Lloyd grew up in Zimbabwe and moved to the United Kingdom fifteen years ago, where he has been based for most of that time in and near Edinburgh, Scotland. Lloyd has a passion for revival and for the local and national church to experience a depth and intimacy in their relationship with Christ fueled and sustained by prayer. Over the last few years Lloyd has been heavily involved with workplace evangelism which led to the prayer initiative known as the 'Concert of Prayer for Scotland' where God led him to gather Christians of many denominations to 'cry out mightily' for the cities and nation of Scotland.

The Concert of Prayer for Scotland

concertofprayerforscotland@gmail.com

FACEBOOK

@concertofprayerforscotland

Twitter

@prayerconcerted

Instagram

@concertofprayerforscotland

Printed in the United States
by Baker & Taylor Publisher Services